Map Skills for Today

Grade 6

All Around the World

Map Skills for Today
All Around the World
Grade 6

Publisher: Keith Garton
Editorial Director: Maureen Hunter-Bone
Editorial Development: Summer Street Press, LLC
Writer: Steve Sheinkin
Project Editor: Miriam Aronin
Editor: Alex Giannini
Design and Production: Dinardo Design, LLC
Photo Editor: Kim Babbitt

Illustration Credits: Stephanie Powers
Map Credits: Mapping Specialists, Ltd.
Photo Credits: Page 5: Super Stock; Page 7: Hulton Archive/Getty Images; Page 11: Lynn Teo Simarski/NSF; Page 13: Ablestock/Jupiter Images; Page 17: Photos.com, Eduardo Garcia/Getty Images; Page 19: Jupiter Images, Photos.com; Page 20: Photodisc/Getty Images; Page 23: Photos.com, AP Images; Page 25: Jupiter Images; Page 27: Daryl Balfour/ Getty Images, Sylvain Grandadam/Getty Images; Page 28: Frans Lemmens/ Getty Images, Vanderharst/Getty Images, Tom Brakefield/Getty Images; Page 33: Jimmy Chin/Getty Images, Digital Vision/Getty Images, Theo Allofs/zefa/Corbis; Page 37: iStock

Teachers: Go online to www.scholastic.com/mapskillsfortoday for teaching ideas and the answer key.

ISBN: 978-1-338-21493-2

1 2 3 4 5 6 7 8 9 10   40   23 22 21 20 19 18

All Around the World

Table of Contents

Hemispheres and Continents

Hemispheres

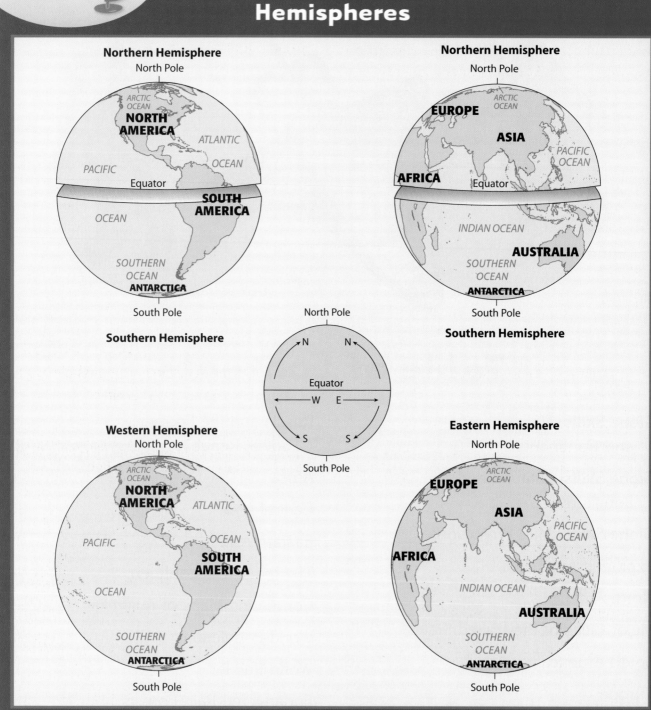

A **globe** is the most accurate map of the Earth. It is a small model of our planet. Like the Earth, a globe is shaped like a ball, or sphere. A globe has several important points and lines. The point at the top of the globe is the North Pole. Another point, the South Pole, is directly opposite the North Pole. The two **poles** are the farthest north and south points on a globe.

Hemispheres

The **equator** is an imaginary line that circles Earth halfway between the North and South poles. The equator divides Earth into half spheres, or **hemispheres**. They are called the Northern and Southern hemispheres.

The equator serves as the dividing line when Earth is divided into Northern and Southern hemispheres. Earth can also be divided into Eastern and Western hemispheres.

Continents

Continents are the largest land areas on Earth. Locate the continents on the globes on page 4. The world's continents can be grouped into those of the Eastern and Western hemisphere. As you can see on the globes on page 4, Europe, Asia, Africa, and Australia are located in the Eastern Hemisphere. North America and South America are in the Western Hemisphere. Antarctica has land in both the Eastern and Western hemispheres.

Use Your Skills

1. If you travel toward the North Pole, your direction is _____ .

2. As you face the North Pole, the direction to your left is _____ .

3. The _____ divides the Earth into Northern and Southern hemispheres.

4. Which ocean is north of North America, Asia, and Europe? _____

5. Which two continents are located completely within the Northern Hemisphere?

   _____

   _____

6. Which continents have land in both the Northern and Southern Hemispheres?

   _____

   _____

Think It Over

If you are at the North Pole, is it possible to go farther north on the Earth? Explain.

A photo of Earth from space

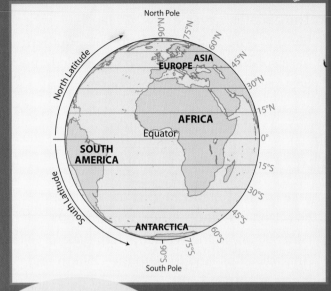

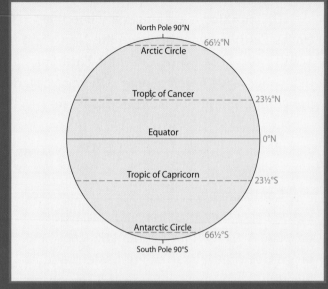

Globe Skills

Latitude and Longitude

To help us locate places on Earth, mapmakers have drawn two sets of imaginary lines on maps and globes. One set of lines runs east and west. These lines are called **parallels**, or lines of **latitude**. The equator, for example, is a parallel. Other parallels measure distances either north or south of the equator. These distances are measured in degrees (°). The equator is at 0° latitude. The North Pole is at 90° north latitude, or 90°N. The South Pole is at 90° south latitude, or 90°S. There are other special parallels. The **Arctic Circle** and the **Tropic of Cancer** are north of the equator. The **Antarctic Circle** and the **Tropic of Capricorn** are south of the equator.

The second set of lines runs north and south. These are called lines of **longitude**, or **meridians**. Meridians measure distance east or west of the **prime meridian**, the meridian that runs through Greenwich, England.

The prime meridian is at 0° longitude. East longitude extends to the east of the prime meridian. West longitude extends to the west of the prime meridian. Both east and west longitudes extend half of the way around the Earth. Because there are 180° in a half circle, there are 180° of west longitude and 180° of east longitude. On a globe or world map, 180° west longitude and 180° east longitude are represented by the same line.

When lines of longitude and latitude are put together, they form a pattern called a **grid**. Using the global grid, we can describe the location of any place in the world by giving its latitude and longitude. For example, what part of the world is located at a latitude of 15°N and a longitude of 15°W? To figure this out, use the grid to find the spot where these two lines cross. On the grid on page 7, you can see that the lines 15°N and 15°W cross in western Africa.

Meridians

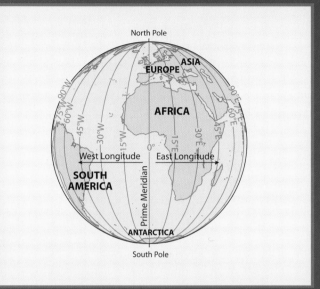

Global Grid

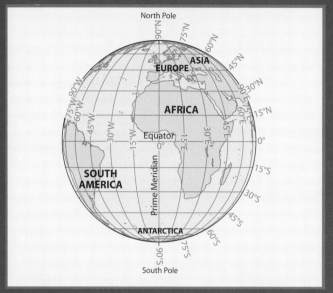

Use Your Skills

1. In degrees, what is the Earth's farthest point south? _____

2. If you were at 60°N, how many degrees south is the equator? _____

3. Which special parallel is found at 66½°N? _____

4. If you were at the Tropic of Capricorn, how many degrees north would you need to travel to reach the equator? _____

5. From the Tropic of Cancer, how many degrees south would you need to travel to reach the South Pole? _____

6. What is the approximate longitude of the western tip of Africa? _____

7. If you were at 45°N and 60°E, you would be on the continent of _____ .

8. If you were at 15°S and 60°W, you would be on the continent of _____ .

9. The equator and prime meridian meet closest to the continent of _____ .

Your Turn Now

Use a globe or map to find the latitude and longitude of your community.

The prime meridian mark in Greenwich, England

Mercator Projection

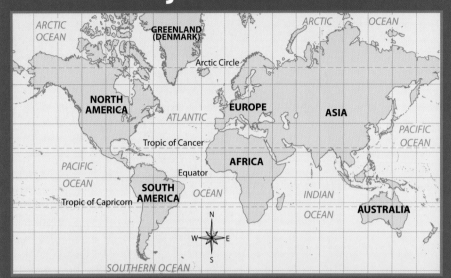

Advantage:
Shapes of land areas and the true direction between any two points are shown correctly.

Disadvantage:
Size of land areas and distances becomes more distorted as you move farther from the equator. Greenland is not this big!

Robinson Projection

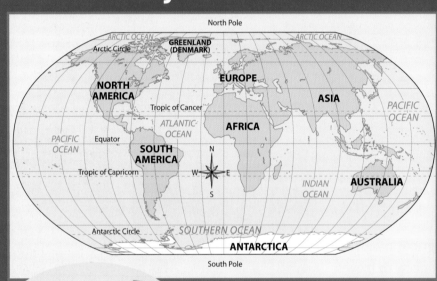

Advantage:
Almost as good as a globe at showing the true size of land and water areas.

Disadvantage:
Shapes of some land areas are badly distorted.

Globe Skills

Map Projections

As you have read, a globe is the most accurate map of Earth—because it is shaped like Earth. Flat maps, on the other hand, can never show the entire surface of the round Earth with perfect accuracy. To see this for yourself, try drawing a perfectly accurate map of an entire baseball or soccer ball on a flat sheet of paper!

Mapmakers have found several ways to **project**, or show, the curved surface of Earth onto a flat map. Each **projection** is more accurate in some ways and less accurate in others. For example, one mapmaker may choose a projection that shows directions most accurately. Another may choose a projection that shows the sizes and shapes of land areas best. Four different types of map projections are shown on the maps above. Each projection includes notes about its advantages and disadvantages.

Interrupted Projection

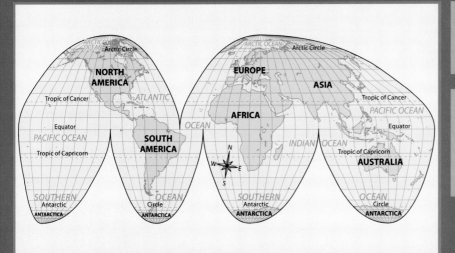

Advantage:
Accurately shows the shapes and sizes of places.

Disadvantage:
Distance and direction are distorted, and some land and water areas are split up, or interrupted.

Equidistant Projection: North Polar Projection

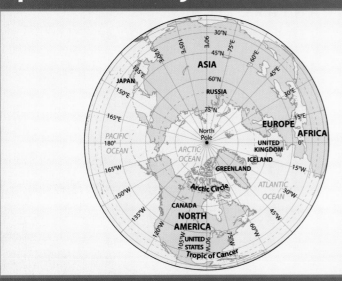

Advantage:
Shows land masses and water in relation to a central point—in this case, the North Pole. Good for determining distances from this center point.

Disadvantage:
Distortion of the shape and size of land areas increases as you move away from the center point.

Use Your Skills

Which map projection would you use for each of the following purposes:

1. To find the shortest route from the North Pole to Europe: _____

2. To find the correct direction from Africa to North America: _____

3. To compare the sizes of North America and South America: _____

4. To find the correct shape and size of Australia: _____

 ## Think It Over

From the North Pole, in which direction would you travel to reach Russia? In which direction would you travel to reach the United States? Use the North Polar projection to help you figure this out.

Exploring Antarctica

Antarctic Explorations

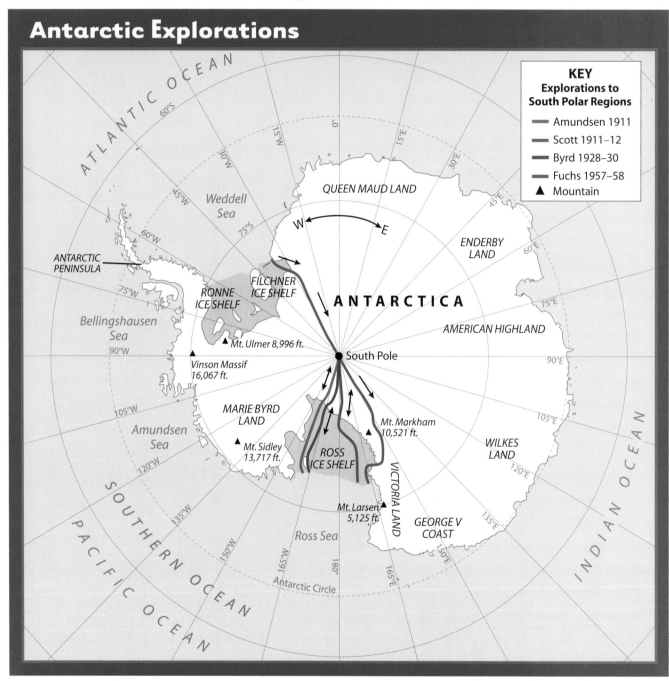

KEY
Explorations to South Polar Regions
- Amundsen 1911
- Scott 1911–12
- Byrd 1928–30
- Fuchs 1957–58
- ▲ Mountain

The continent of Antarctica is the coldest place in the world, with temperatures typically dropping to -100°F or colder. Even in the Antarctic summer, temperatures rarely rise above freezing. Antarctica is also the driest continent, receiving less than an inch of snow a year. It is actually a frozen desert. Since the little snow that falls each year never melts, the snow has collected over the years and pressure has turned it into a massive ice sheet. The Antarctic ice sheet holds about 70 percent of the world's fresh water.

The Antarctica map above is a South Polar projection. This is the view you would have if you picked up a globe and looked at it from underneath, with the South Pole directly above your eyes.

Antarctic Explorers

Daring explorers have made great contributions to our knowledge of Antarctica. In 1911 two groups of explorers set out from the Ross Ice Shelf on a race to the South Pole. A group led by Norwegian Roald Amundsen reached the pole just a month ahead of a group headed by British explorer Robert Falcon Scott. Scott and his fellow explorers died trying to return.

The most important American explorer was Richard E. Byrd. During his 1928–1930 expedition to Antarctica, Byrd became the second person to fly an airplane across the South Pole. Having already flown over the North Pole, he became the first person to fly over both poles. Between 1957 and 1958, English explorer Vivian Fuchs became the first person to cross the continent by land.

 ## Use Your Skills

1. Which explorer was the first to reach the South Pole? _____

2. Which exploration did not begin on the Ross Sea? _____

3. If you were at the South Pole, you would need to travel _____ to reach American Highland.

4. The portion of Antarctica that extends the farthest north is _____ .

5. If your position were 75°S and 90°W, you would be near _____ .

Your Turn Now

Using the library or Internet, find out more about one of the famous Antarctic explorers. Write a one-page report about this person's adventures. Be sure to include a map of Antarctica, showing the route taken by this explorer.

Although Antarctica has no permanent population, scientists from around the world have established research bases on the continent.

THE UNITED STATES OF AMERICA
WELCOMES YOU TO
AMUNDSEN – SCOTT SOUTH POLE STATION

North America

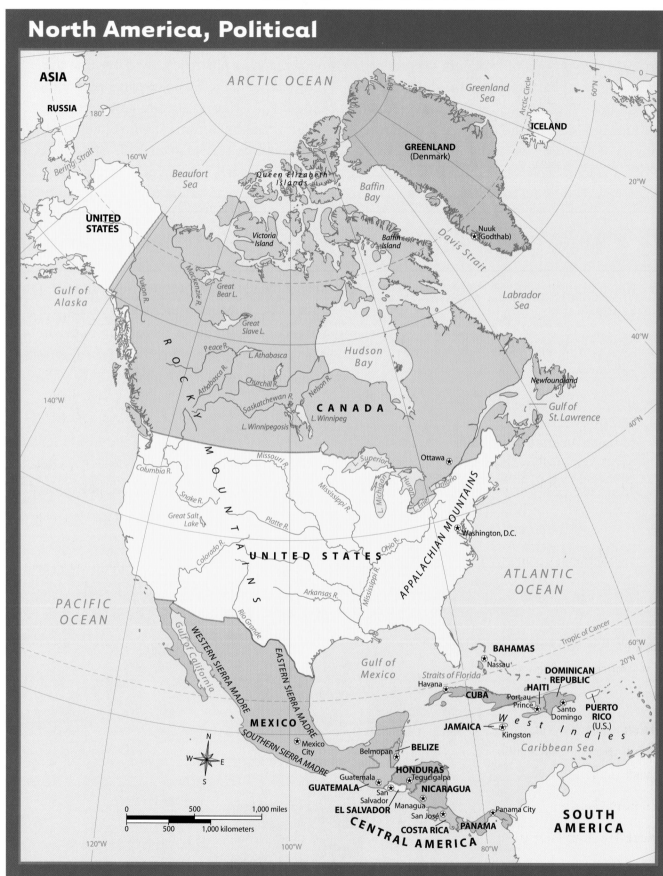

North America is the third-largest continent in terms of land area. Canada, the United States, and Mexico are by far the continent's largest countries. North America also includes the nations of Central America, and island nations of the Caribbean, which are known as the West Indies. Greenland, the world's largest island, is a territory of Denmark.

Rocky Mountains
Caribbean Beach

 Use Your Skills

1. What mountain range is east of the Ohio River? _____

2. What Canadian lake lies partly within the Arctic Circle? _____

3. What body of water separates Florida from Cuba? _____

4. Which mountain range is directly east of the Gulf of California? _____
_____

5. _____ is the capital of the southernmost country in North America.

6. Two rivers that flow into the Gulf of Mexico are the _____ and the
_____.

7. Using lines of latitude and longitude, locate each place listed in the left-hand column below. Write the number of the place that matches each location.

____ a. $66\frac{1}{2}$°N 170°W   1. Great Bear Lake
____ b. 10°N 85°W   2. Washington, D.C.
____ c. $66\frac{1}{2}$°N 120°W   3. Great Salt Lake
____ d. 42°N 114°W   4. Bering Strait
____ e. 39°N 77°W   5. Costa Rica

 Your Turn Now

Use an encyclopedia or the Internet to research the information needed to complete the information box below.

Key Facts About North America
Area: 9,365,000 square miles
Population: 515,000,000
Most Populous City: _____   population: _____

Largest Country: _____   square miles: _____

Most Populous Country: _____   population: _____

Tallest Mountain: _____   height: _____

Major Cities of the United States

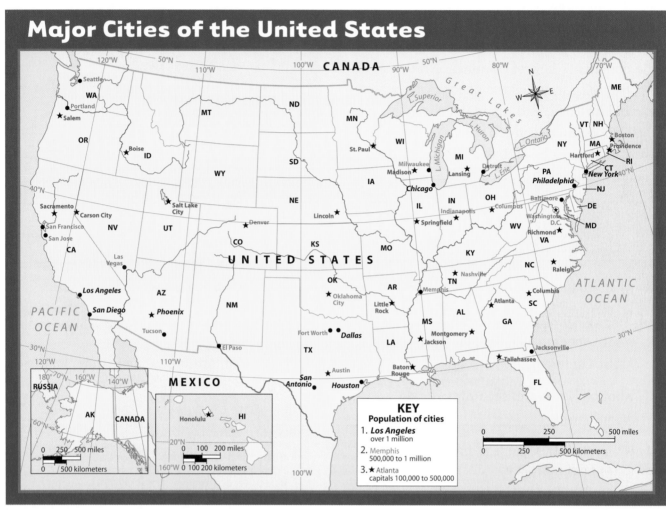

Major Cities of the United States

KEY
Population of cities
1. *Los Angeles* — over 1 million
2. Memphis — 500,000 to 1 million
3. ★ Atlanta — capitals 100,000 to 500,000

Use Your Skills

1. The state of _____ has the most cities with populations over 1 million.

2. The United States has _____ cities with populations of more than 1 million.

3. In states bordering the Pacific Ocean, the state with the most cities of 500,000 or more is _____ .

4. _____ is the only city on the Great Lakes with more than 1 million people.

5. Which of these states has the capital city with the biggest population: Georgia, Ohio, or Mississippi? _____

6. Use the map and map key above to help you rank these cities 1–3, with 1 being the most populous and 3 being the least populous.

_____ St. Paul, MN   _____ Jacksonville, FL

_____ Los Angeles, CA

Think It Over

What are some conclusions you can draw about the location of the biggest cities in the United States? What geographical factors seem to be linked to the development of large cities?

Fastest Growing U.S. Cities

 Map It!

You may not have heard of most of the cities listed in the table on this page. But in 2006 these were the 10 fastest-growing cities of 100,000 or more people. Your job will be to label these cities on the United States map above. In the table you will see that each city has a rank. These numbers match the numbers on the map. For example, Irvine is ranked 10 on the table. Find 10 on the map above. This is the location of Irvine. Write in the city name. Then fill in the rest of the map, adding the names of the other nine cities in the table. Complete the table by writing in the name of the state in which each city is located.

Rank	City	State	Percent Growth in Past Year
1	Elk Grove		11.6%
2	North Las Vegas		11.4%
3	Port St. Lucie		11.0%
4	Gilbert		11.0%
5	Cape Coral		9.2%
6	Moreno Valley		7.3%
7	Rancho Cucamonga		6.4%
8	Miramar		5.2%
9	Chandler		4.9%
10	Irvine		4.9%

 Think It Over

What conclusions can you draw about the locations of the fastest-growing American cities? What is one thing these locations have in common? What might be one factor affecting this pattern of growth?

South America

South America, Political

Caribbean Sea

Barranquilla
Maracaibo
Caracas ⊛

CENTRAL AMERICA

10°N

VENEZUELA

Georgetown ⊛
Paramaribo

ATLANTIC OCEAN

Medellín
Bogotá ⊛

GUYANA
SURINAME

Cayenne

Cali •

COLOMBIA

FRENCH GUIANA (FRANCE)

Rio Magdalena
Rio Orinoco

Equator 0°

Quito ⊛

ECUADOR

A M A Z O N

Amazon R.
Amazon R.

Marajo Island

Equator 0°

Guayaquil
Gulf of Guayaquil

B A S I N

Rio Madeira
Rio Xingu

AMAZON RAIN FOREST

Recife

10°S

A
N
D
E
S

Lima ⊛

PERU

B R A Z I L

Rio Araguaia
Rio Tocantins
Rio São Francisco

Salvador

Lake Titicaca

La Paz

Brasilia ⊛

M
O
U
N
T
A
I
N
S

BOLIVIA

20°S

Sucre ⊛

Belo Horizonte

ATACAMA DESERT

PARAGUAY

Rio Paraná

Tropic of Capricorn

Rio de Janeiro

São Paulo

Tropic of Capricorn

Asunción ⊛

Curitiba

ARGENTINA

Rio Paraguay
Rio Uruguay

Pôrto Alegre

30°S

Córdoba •

URUGUAY

30°S

CHILE

Parana •

Santiago ⊛

Buenos Aires ⊛

Montevideo

PAMPAS

Rio de la Plata

PACIFIC OCEAN

N
W   E
S

40°S

Gulf of San Matias

40°S

PATAGONIA

Gulf of San Jorge

KEY
Population of cities

1. *Rio de Janeiro*
over 2 million

0   250   500 miles
0   250   500 kilometers

50°S

Falkland Islands (U.K.)

2. Cordoba
500,000 to 2 million

3. ⊛ Georgetown
capitals over 100,000

Strait of Magellan

South Georgia Island (U.K.)

4. ⊛ Cayenne
capitals 25,000 to 100,000

Tierra del Fuego

Cape Horn

South America is the fourth-largest continent. Like North America, South America has diverse climates, landforms, and people. Eight South American nations are home to parts of the Amazon Rain Forest, the largest rain forest in the world. Much of South America belonged to Spain until the early 1800s, which explains why Spanish is the primary language in most South American countries. Portuguese is spoken in Brazil, which was a colony of Portugal.

 ## Use Your Skills

1. South America is mainly in the _____ and _____ Hemispheres.

2. Brazil shares a border with every South American country except _____ and _____ .

3. The _____ Mountains cover much of western South America.

4. At its widest point, Chile is about _____ miles wide.

5. The South American capital city located closest to the equator is _____ , which is the capital of _____ .

6. Locate and number on the map one example of each of the following places.
    1. a strait
    2. a cape
    3. a national border formed by a river
    4. an island owned by Great Britain
    5. a capital city with more than 2 million people

Amazon River

Andes Mountains, Peru

Rio de Janeiro, Brazil

Your Turn Now

Which South American country would you most like to visit? Choose one country and use the Internet or library to find some interesting facts about the country. Then on a sheet of paper make a box of interesting facts about the country. You may want to include some photographs along with your fact box. Share your fact boxes with other students.

Europe

Europe, Political

Greenland (Denmark)

Greenland Sea

0 250 500 miles
0 250 500 kilometers

Arctic Circle

ICELAND
Reykjavik

Barents Sea

Norwegian Sea

ATLANTIC OCEAN

North Sea

SWEDEN

FINLAND

Lake Onega

NORWAY

Helsinki

Oslo

Stockholm

Tallinn
ESTONIA

Lake Ladoga

RUSSIA

Moscow

Volga R.

Riga
LATVIA

DENMARK

Copenhagen

Baltic Sea

LITHUANIA
Vilnius

Minsk

RUSSIA

BELARUS

Dublin
IRELAND

UNITED KINGDOM

NETHERLANDS
Amsterdam

Berlin

Warsaw

Kiev

Dnieper R.

London

Brussels

Rhine R.

GERMANY

POLAND

UKRAINE

Celtic Sea

BELGIUM

Luxembourg

Prague
CZECH REPUBLIC

SLOVAKIA

MOLDOVA

Paris

LUXEMBOURG

LIECHTENSTEIN

Vienna

Bratislava

Chisinau

Vaduz

Budapest

Bern
SWITZERLAND

AUSTRIA

HUNGARY

ROMANIA

Bay of Biscay

FRANCE

Ljubljana
SLOVENIA

CROATIA
Zagreb

Belgrade

Bucharest

Black Sea

Danube R.

ITALY

BOSNIA & HERZEGOVINA

SERBIA

Monaco

Sarajevo

Andorra-la Vella

SAN MARINO

San Marino

MONTENEGRO

Pristina
KOSOVO

Sofia

BULGARIA

TURKEY

PORTUGAL

ANDORRA

MONACO

Podgorica

Tirana

MACEDONIA

Skopje

40°N

Madrid

Rome

VATICAN CITY

ALBANIA

GREECE

ASIA

Lisbon

SPAIN

Aegean Sea

Athens

Valletta **MALTA**

AFRICA

Mediterranean Sea

Europe is the second-smallest continent —only Australia is smaller. Though it is only about half the size of South America, Europe is home to nearly as many people as North and South America combined. Within Europe's relatively small land area are more than 40 countries and hundreds of ethnic groups.

Use Your Skills

1. The sea between Ukraine and Turkey is called the _____ .

2. The _____ Sea is crossed by the prime meridian (0° longitude) and is north of 60°N.

3. The nations located on a peninsula southwest of France are _____ and _____ .

4. The city of Warsaw is the capital of _____ .

5. The island nation just south of the Arctic Circle is called _____ .

6. The country whose southern border touches Germany is _____ .

7. Two European countries that border only one other country are _____ and _____ .

8. The capital of Russia is _____ . It is located about_____ miles from London, which is the capital of _____ .

 ## Think It Over

What problems could occur on a continent that has so many countries within such a small space? What might be some of the benefits?

 ## Your Turn Now

Look up the European Union on the Internet. Write a short report describing the main goals of this organization. What challenges does it face? Include a list of member nations.

Roman Forum and Temple of Saturn ruins, Rome, Italy

Arc de Triomphe, Paris, France

Tower Bridge, London, United Kingdom

Dunluce Castle, County Antrim, Northern Ireland

Mediterranean Lands

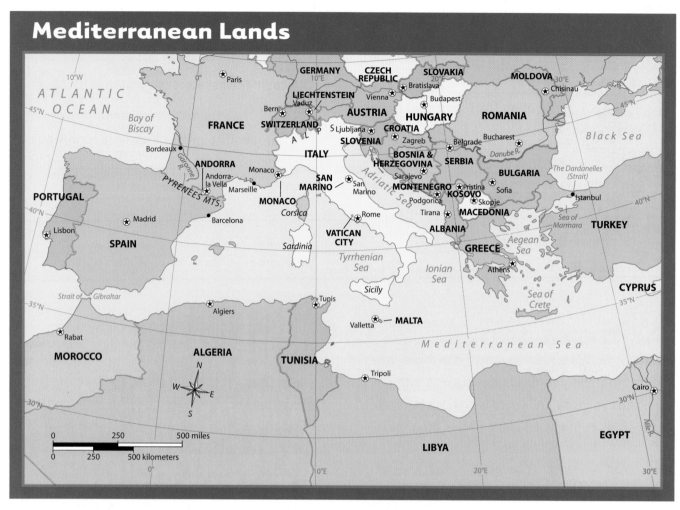

Mediterranean Lands

The Mediterranean is the world's second largest sea—only the Caribbean is larger. The Mediterranean is connected to the Atlantic Ocean by the Strait of Gibraltar, which is just eight miles wide at its narrowest point. More than 20 nations in Europe, Asia, and Africa have land bordering the Mediterranean.

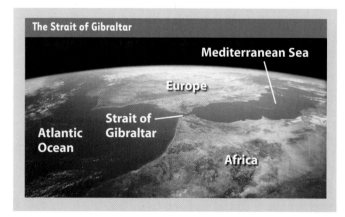

The Strait of Gibraltar

Mediterranean Sea
Europe
Strait of Gibraltar
Atlantic Ocean
Africa

Use Your Skills

Complete each sentence with NE, SE, NW, or SW.

1. Albania's capital is _____ of Switzerland's capital.

2. Algeria's capital is _____ of Morocco's capital.

3. Marseille, France, is _____ of Barcelona, Spain.

Write the name of the place that is described

4. country at 35°N 10°E _____

5. city at 45°N 20°E _____

6. island at 40°N 8°E _____

Mediterranean Travels

A map of the Mediterranean region showing countries of Europe, North Africa, and the Middle East. Labels on the map include:

ATLANTIC OCEAN, Bay of Biscay, PORTUGAL, SPAIN, Strait of Gibraltar, MOROCCO, ALGERIA, TUNISIA, Tripoli, LIBYA, FRANCE, Bordeaux, Garonne R., ANDORRA, MONACO, Corsica, Sardinia, SAN MARINO, VATICAN CITY, ITALY, ALPS, SWITZERLAND, Bern, LIECHTENSTEIN, GERMANY, CZECH REPUBLIC, AUSTRIA, SLOVENIA, CROATIA, HUNGARY, SLOVAKIA, MOLDOVA, ROMANIA, BOSNIA & HERZEGOVINA, SERBIA, Danube R., BULGARIA, MONTENEGRO, KOSOVO, MACEDONIA, ALBANIA, GREECE, Tyrrhenian Sea, Sicily, MALTA, Ionian Sea, Adriatic Sea, Aegean Sea, Sea of Crete, Sea of Marmara, The Dardanelles (Strait), Istanbul, TURKEY, Black Sea, CYPRUS, Mediterranean Sea, EGYPT, Nile R.

Scale: 0 – 250 – 500 miles; 0 – 250 – 500 kilometers

Map It!

Use the map above to plan several trips around the Mediterranean region. After figuring out a route for each trip, you will draw the route on the map.

1. Beginning in Tripoli, Libya, you want to travel to Bern, Switzerland.

You begin by sailing _____ across the _____ Sea.

One country in Europe you have to go through is Italy.

A mountain range you will cross is the

_____ .

Now draw your route on the map above.

2. Beginning in Bordeaux, France, you want to travel to Istanbul, Turkey, completely by water. You begin by sailing northwest on the Garonne River. Then your route takes you over the following waterways:

bay _____

ocean _____

strait _____

four seas _____

strait _____

Now draw your route on the map above.

3. Now choose a trip you would like to take in this region. Make sure it is more than 1,000 miles. Draw the cities you would like to visit and your route on the map above. Describe your trip.

21

The Middle East

The Middle East, Political

The region known as the Middle East is the birthplace of three of the world's major religions: Christianity, Islam, and Judaism. In recent decades, conflicts over religion and land have created problems in the Middle East. Jewish and Muslim neighbors have fought over land since Israel became an independent nation in 1948.

Control of the area's rich oil resources and global terrorist activities have been other sources of conflict. Armed forces from the United States and other countries overthrew Iraq's dictator Saddam Hussein in 2003. The United States and its allies then began the long, difficult process of helping to rebuild the nation.

1. Which body of water is directly north of Muscat, Oman? _____

2. What river flows through Egypt and Sudan? _____

3. The capital of Iraq is _____ .
It is located along the _____
River.

4. To travel from Eritrea to Saudi Arabia, which body of water would you need to cross? _____

5. What is the capital of the island that is west of Syria and south of Turkey? _____

6. What is the largest country on the largest peninsula in the Middle East? _____

7. Which of these statements can you prove about Turkey using only the map on page 22? Circle the letter on each statement you can prove from this map.

   A. Its water boundaries are longer than its land boundaries.
   B. It has mountain ranges in the south and east.
   C. Ankara is its largest city.

8. Give the approximate latitude and longitude of the following places. The first one is done for you.

   Damascus, Syria __34° N / 36° E__

   Sanaa, Yemen _____

   Tel Aviv, Israel _____

   Abu Dhabi, U.A.E. _____

   Tehran, Iran _____

 Your Turn Now

Find out more about one ongoing conflict in the Middle East. Write a short report giving a summary of this conflict. What are the main causes of the conflict? What are some possible solutions? Which solution do you think might work?

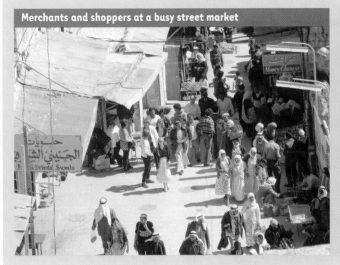
Merchants and shoppers at a busy street market

Oil workers at an oil installation in Iraq

Oil Fields and Pipelines

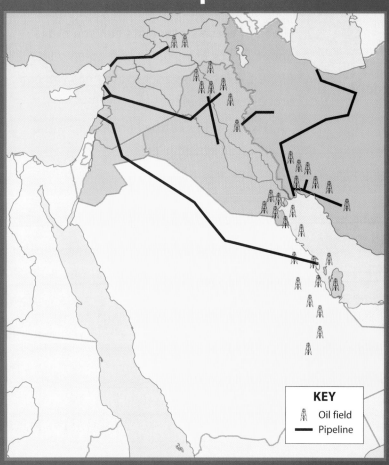

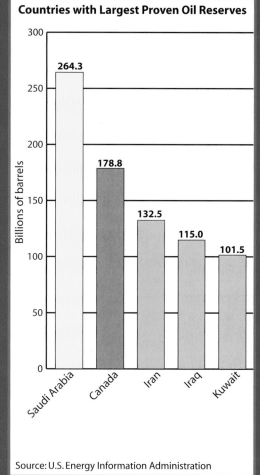

Countries with Largest Proven Oil Reserves

Saudi Arabia	264.3
Canada	178.8
Iran	132.5
Iraq	115.0
Kuwait	101.5

Billions of barrels

KEY

🛢 Oil field
— Pipeline

Source: U.S. Energy Information Administration

 Map It!

Many of the world's oil-rich nations are located in the Middle East. The map above shows some of the major oil fields and pipelines in the region. Complete the map above by filling in the names of the countries and bodies of water shown. Use the map of the Middle East on page 22 as a reference. Then use your completed map, along with the graph above, to answer the following questions.

1. An oil pipeline beginning in eastern Saudi Arabia crosses the countries of _____

_____

_____ before reaching

the _____ Sea.

2. The map above shows that much of the world's oil is found in fields around this body of water: _____ .

3. Of the five nations with the largest oil reserves, _____ are located in the Middle East. They are: _____

_____ .

 Think It Over

The map above shows that many oil pipelines carry oil to large bodies of water. What do you think is the reason for this?

24

Russia and the Former Soviet Republics

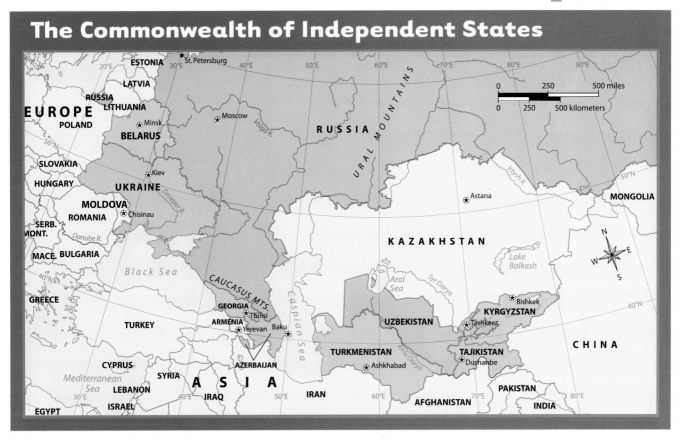

The Commonwealth of Independent States

When the Soviet Union collapsed in 1991, former Soviet republics declared their independence. Russia and 11 former Soviet republics joined in the Commonwealth of Independent States (CIS), a loose federation of nations. The goal of the CIS is to encourage member nations to cooperate in areas such as foreign policy, defense, and trade. Three former republics of the Soviet Union—Estonia, Latvia, and Lithuania—chose to become part of the European Union rather than the CIS.

Moscow, Russia

Use Your Skills

1. Which capital city is just north of the Iranian border? _____

2. What is the second-largest nation in the CIS? _____

3. Where is St. Petersburg in relation to Moscow? _____

4. Which CIS nations border Russia? _____

_____

_____

5. The _____ form the northern border of Georgia and Azerbaijan.

6. The capital of Kazakhstan is about _____ miles from Moscow.

Africa

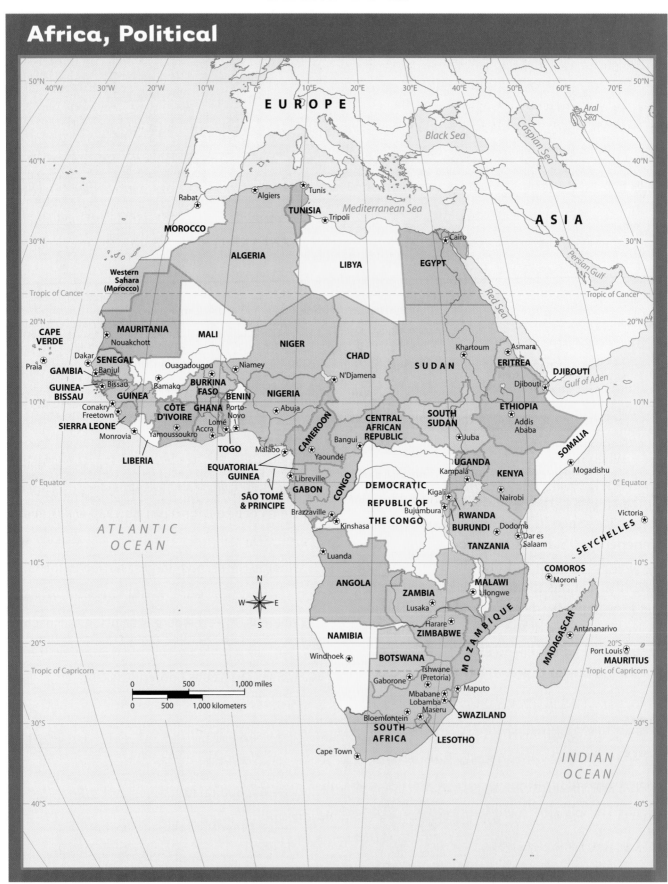

Africa, Political

EUROPE

Black Sea

Mediterranean Sea

ASIA

Aral Sea

Caspian Sea

Persian Gulf

Rabat ⚉
Algiers ⚉
Tunis ⚉
TUNISIA
Tripoli ⚉

MOROCCO

ALGERIA

LIBYA

EGYPT
Cairo ⚉

Red Sea

Tropic of Cancer

Western
Sahara
(Morocco)

**CAPE
VERDE**

Praia ⚉

MAURITANIA
Nouakchott ⚉

MALI

NIGER

CHAD

SUDAN
Khartoum ⚉

Asmara ⚉
ERITREA

DJIBOUTI
Djibouti ⚉

Gulf of Aden

Dakar ⚉
SENEGAL
GAMBIA ⚉ Banjul

Ouagadougou ⚉
Niamey ⚉
N'Djamena ⚉

**GUINEA-
BISSAU** ⚉ Bissau
Bamako ⚉
**BURKINA
FASO**
BENIN

NIGERIA

Abuja ⚉

Bangui ⚉

**CENTRAL
AFRICAN
REPUBLIC**

**SOUTH
SUDAN**
Juba ⚉

ETHIOPIA
Addis
Ababa ⚉

SOMALIA

Conakry ⚉
Freetown ⚉
GUINEA
**CÔTE
D'IVOIRE**
GHANA
Porto-
Novo ⚉
Lomé ⚉
Accra ⚉

SIERRA LEONE
Monrovia ⚉
Yamoussoukro ⚉

TOGO
Malabo ⚉
CAMEROON
Yaoundé ⚉

LIBERIA

**EQUATORIAL
GUINEA**
Libreville ⚉

**SÃO TOMÉ
& PRINCIPE**

GABON
Brazzaville ⚉
Kinshasa ⚉

CONGO

**DEMOCRATIC
REPUBLIC OF
THE CONGO**

Kampala ⚉
UGANDA
Kigali ⚉
Bujumbura ⚉
RWANDA
BURUNDI
Dodoma ⚉

KENYA
Nairobi ⚉

Mogadishu ⚉

0° Equator

Victoria ⚉

SEYCHELLES

ATLANTIC
OCEAN

Luanda ⚉

Dar es
Salaam ⚉
TANZANIA

COMOROS
Moroni ⚉

ANGOLA

ZAMBIA
Lusaka ⚉

Harare ⚉
ZIMBABWE

MALAWI
Lilongwe ⚉

MOZAMBIQUE

MADAGASCAR
Antananarivo ⚉

Port Louis ⚉
MAURITIUS

Tropic of Capricorn

NAMIBIA

Windhoek ⚉

BOTSWANA
Gaborone ⚉
Tshwane
(Pretoria) ⚉
Maputo ⚉

Mbabane ⚉
Lobamba
Maseru ⚉
SWAZILAND

Bloemfontein ⚉
**SOUTH
AFRICA**
LESOTHO

Cape Town ⚉

INDIAN
OCEAN

N
W ✦ E
S

0   500   1,000 miles
0   500   1,000 kilometers

Africa is the second-largest continent—second only to Asia. The equator runs through the center of Africa. Most of the continent lies in the tropical region, the region between the Tropic of Cancer and the Tropic of Capricorn. Most African nations are categorized as "developing nations," or nations with little industry and a relatively low standard of living. Many of these nations have great potential, however, because they are rich in natural resources including oil and precious metals.

Mt. Kilimanjaro

Pyramids in Cairo, Egypt

 Use Your Skills

1. Which African nation has coastlines on both the Atlantic and Indian oceans?

   _____

2. The African country that reaches farthest north is _____ .

3. The equator runs through these African nations: _____

   _____ .

4. The longitude line of 50°E runs through the African countries of _____ and _____ .

 Think It Over

Does the prime meridian pass through Africa? How can you tell?

 Your Turn Now

Use the Internet or an encyclopedia to find the information needed to complete the key facts box below.

Key Facts About Africa

Area: _____

Largest Country: _____

Most Populous Country: _____

Tallest Mountain: _____

Two more interesting facts: _____

_____

Population: _____

Square miles: _____

Population: _____

Height: _____

Comparing Maps of Africa

Physical Map of Africa

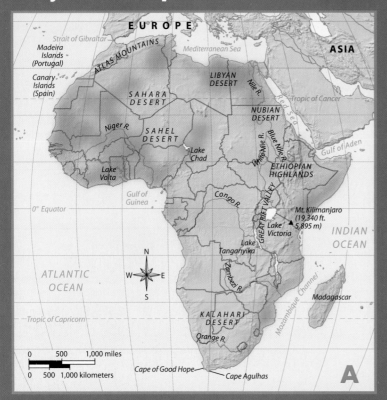

A

The maps on this page give you a lot of information about the landforms and physical features of Africa. The physical map shows major rivers, deserts, and other landforms. The vegetation map shows what types of plants grow naturally in different regions. The Sahara Desert map gives you an idea of how huge the desert is by comparing it to a map of the United States. Use these maps, along with the political map of Africa on page 26, to answer the questions on the next page.

Vegetation Map of Africa

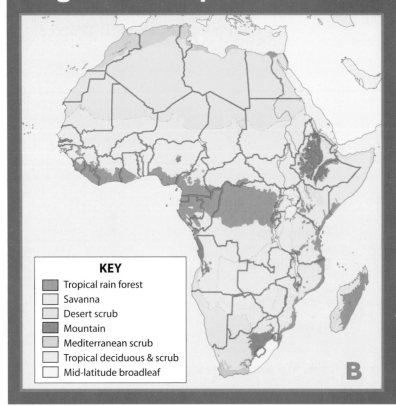

KEY
- Tropical rain forest
- Savanna
- Desert scrub
- Mountain
- Mediterranean scrub
- Tropical deciduous & scrub
- Mid-latitude broadleaf

B

Sahara Desert

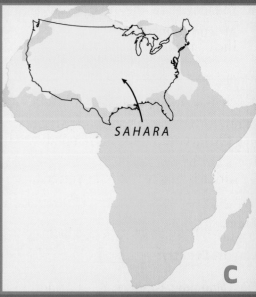

C

The Sahara covers nearly 500,000 square miles. That's more than the 48 connected United States.

1. Lake Victoria is directly _____ of Mt. Kilimanjaro.

2. Much of northern Africa is covered by the _____ .

3. What mountain range stretches across northern Morocco? _____

4. Africa's tropical rain forests are found mainly in the _____ region of the continent.

5. Two vegetation regions through which the Nile River flows are _____ and _____ .

6. The Blue Nile and the White Nile join in _____ and flow north through _____ .

Complete each sentence with a direction (N, S, E, or W) and the name of a large body of water.

7. The Nile River flows _____ into the _____ .

8. The Congo River flows _____ into the _____ .

Which map or maps on page 28 would you use to prove each of the following statements— A, B, or C?

9. Africa is larger than the United States. _____

10. The Atlas Mountains are located northwest of the Sahara. _____

11. Madagascar has three distinct forms of vegetation. _____

12. The Congo River flows through a region of tropical rain forest. _____ and _____

Which country do you think gets more rain, Libya or the Democratic Republic of Congo? Which maps helped you reach this conclusion?

Sahara Desert

Rain forest along the Blue Nile, Ethiopia, Africa

Savanna wildlife

Central Asia

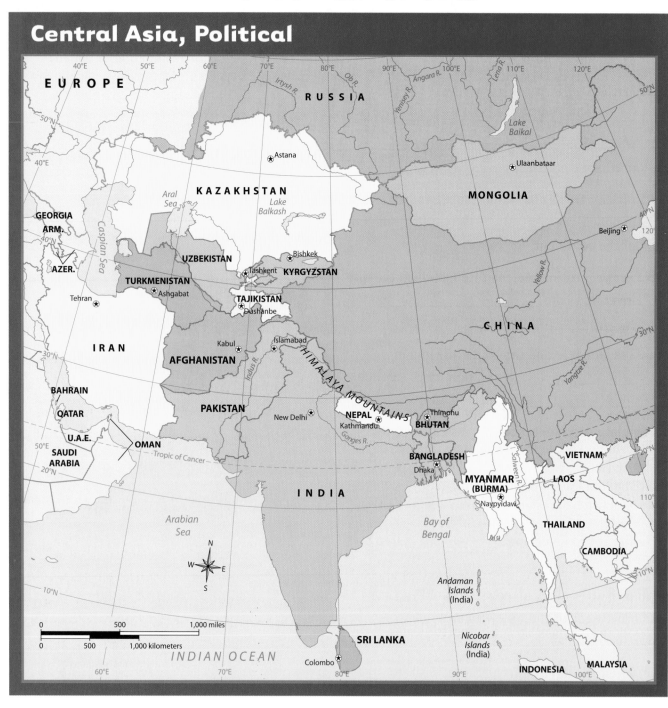

Central Asian nations have been in the news often since September 11, 2001, when al-Qaeda, a terrorist group based in Afghanistan, carried out a massive attack on the United States. Terrorists crashed planes into the World Trade Center in New York City and the Pentagon near Washington, D.C. In response to the attacks, U.S.-led forces invaded Afghanistan. In the years since, some of the terrorists have used the geography of the region to their advantage by hiding in the rugged mountains of Afghanistan and Pakistan. The elevation map on page 31 shows you which parts of Afghanistan are the most mountainous.

Afghanistan, Elevation

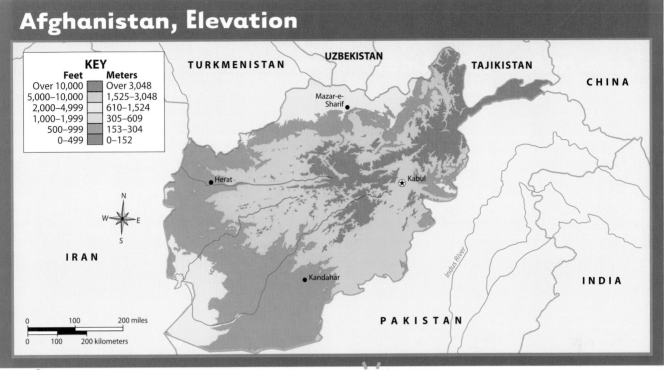

KEY

Feet	Meters
Over 10,000	Over 3,048
5,000–10,000	1,525–3,048
2,000–4,999	610–1,524
1,000–1,999	305–609
500–999	153–304
0–499	0–152

Use Your Skills

Use the maps on pages 30 and 31 to answer these questions.

1. Central Asia is in the _____ and _____ Hemispheres.

2. The continent to the west of Central Asia on this map is _____ .

3. The _____ Sea is surrounded by Uzbekistan and Kazakhstan.

4. Three countries that have parts of the Himalaya Mountains are _____ _____ .

5. The capital of Afghanistan is _____ . It is located between _____ and _____ feet above sea level.

6. One city in Afghanistan that is located at a higher elevation than Kandahar is _____ .

7. Which parts of Afghanistan are the least mountainous? _____ .

Think It Over

What information on the map of Central Asia might explain Nepal's nickname: "the roof of the world"?

Your Turn Now

Many of the world's tallest mountains are located in Central Asia's Himalaya range. Using Internet or encyclopedia sources as a reference, make your own chart of the world's 10 tallest peaks. Include the name and height of each mountain, as well as the country in which it is located. Are all these peaks located in Central Asia?

Eastern Asia

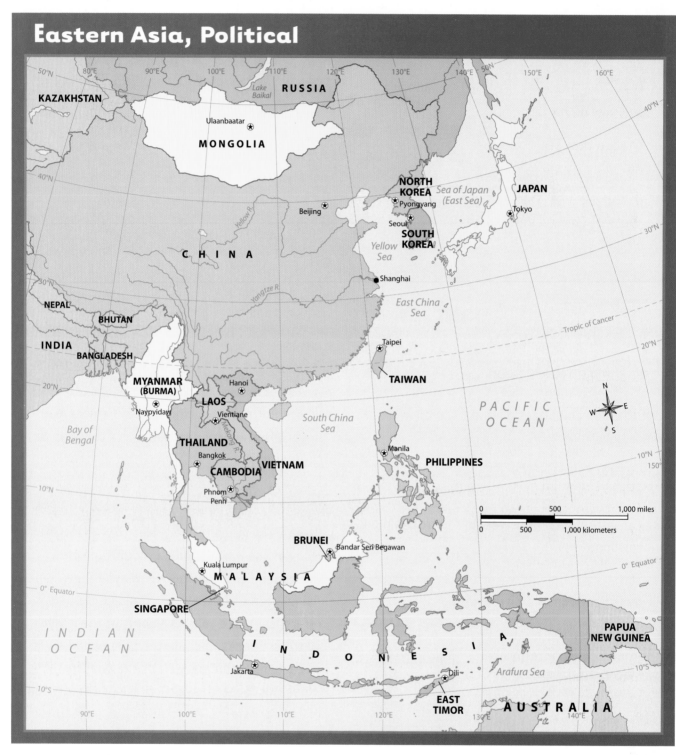

Eastern Asia, Political

Eastern Asia is a large region with a variety of landforms and climates. At the heart of the region is China, which is the world's third-largest nation in land area. Home to about 1.3 billion people, China is also the world's most populous nation.

In fact, about one-fifth of the entire world population lives in China. Two more of the world's ten most populous nations are in East Asia. Indonesia ranks fourth in population, with 232 million people. Japan's population of 127 million is the world's tenth-largest.

 ## Use Your Skills

1. What sea separates China from North and South Korea? _____

2. If you flew from Hanoi to Manila, which sea would you cross? _____

3. The sea that separates Indonesia from Australia is the _____ .

4. Of the Eastern Asian countries on the map south of China, which has no coastline? _____

5. The capital cities of the countries _____ and _____ are located in the Southern Hemisphere.

6. _____ is the northernmost capital in Eastern Asia.

7. The approximate latitude and longitude of the Chinese city of Shanghai is _____ °N and _____ °E.

8. Each year China adds about 12 million new citizens. At that rate, what will its population be in 2050? _____

 ## Think It Over

China has only about 7 percent of the world's arable, or farmable, land and fresh water. What problems might these statistics pose in relation to China's growing population? What solutions might be found?

 ## Your Turn Now

East Asia is home to some very large cities. Use the Internet to find a list of the world's 10 most populous cities. Then create your own chart ranking these 10 cities and their populations. How many of these cities are located in Eastern Asia?

World's Most Populous Cities

	City	Country	Population
1.			
2.			
3.			
4.			
5.			
6.			
7.			
8.			
9.			
10.			

Rural Southeast Asia

Urban Southeast Asia

The Indian Subcontinent

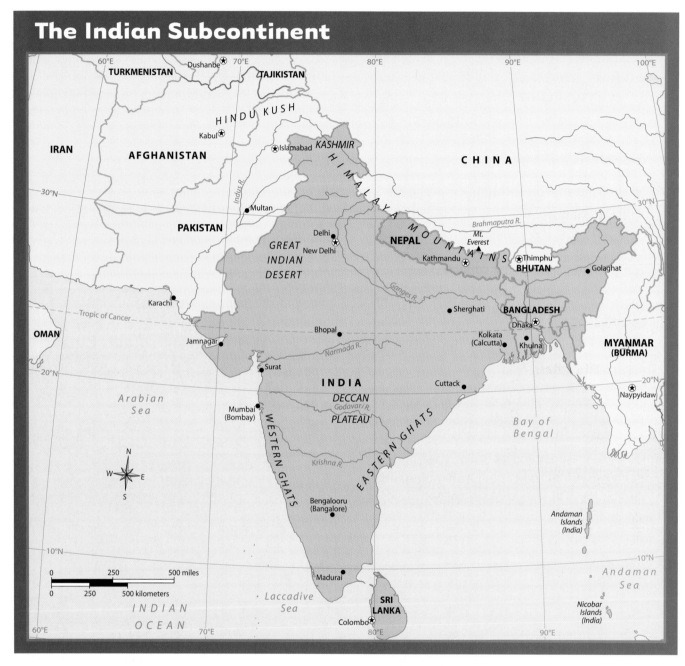

The Indian Subcontinent

A **subcontinent** is a large region of land that is smaller than a continent. The Indian Subcontinent includes India, Pakistan, Bangladesh, Bhutan, Nepal, and Sri Lanka. Although the countries of this region share many geographic and economic similarities, their peoples are very different culturally. These differences have led to problems.

Religious differences, for example, have played a key role in disputes between India and Pakistan. India's main religion is Hinduism. Most Pakistanis are Muslims (members of the Islamic faith). The most serious dispute has been over ownership of the border region of Kashmir. India and Pakistan fought wars over the territory in 1947 and 1965. Tensions remain high. Because both nations have nuclear weapons, all the nations of the world are concerned about this ongoing conflict.

1. Which nation in this region is closest to the equator? _____

2. Bangladesh was part of Pakistan until the 1970s. It was called "East Pakistan." What nation separated the two parts of Pakistan?

_____

3. Mt. Everest, the world's tallest mountain, is near the border of _____

and _____ .

4. Kathmandu, Nepal, is _____ of New Delhi, India.

Religions of the Indian Subcontinent

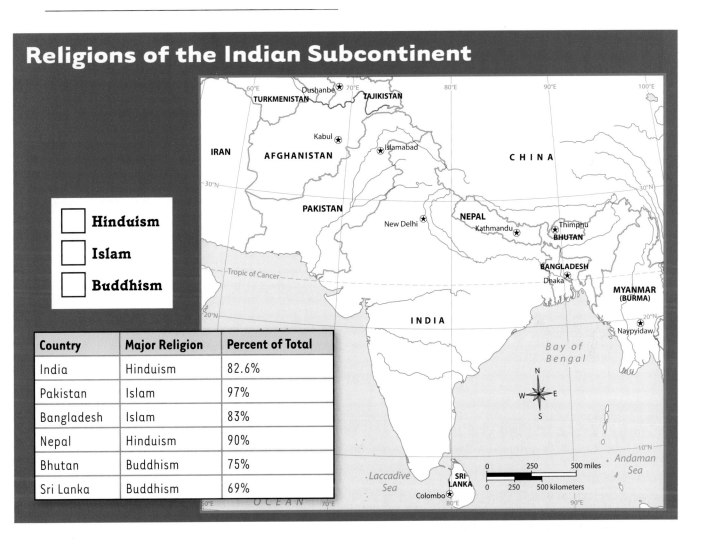

| Hinduism |
| Islam |
| Buddhism |

Country	Major Religion	Percent of Total
India	Hinduism	82.6%
Pakistan	Islam	97%
Bangladesh	Islam	83%
Nepal	Hinduism	90%
Bhutan	Buddhism	75%
Sri Lanka	Buddhism	69%

Map It!

Use the outline map and table above to create a religion map of the Indian Subcontinent. The map shows the nations of the subcontinent. The chart shows the majority religion in each nation. Choose one color for each of the three religions shown on the chart. Then use that color to fill in each nation in which this is the majority religion. Fill in the map key as well, showing which color stands for which religion. What conclusions can you draw from your map?

Comparing Maps of Australia

Australia, Political

KEY
- ✪ National capital
- ★ State, territorial capitals
- • Other cities
- – – State boundaries
- **State names**

INDONESIA · EAST TIMOR · NEW GUINEA

Arafura Sea · Torres Strait · Timor Sea · INDIAN OCEAN · Gulf of Carpentaria · Coral Sea · Great Barrier Reef

Darwin

Derby · Broome · GREAT SANDY DESERT · Tennant Creek · Cairns · Mount Isa · Mackay

Port Hedland · Northern Territory · Queensland

Learmonth · Western Australia · Alice Springs · Rockhampton · Gladstone · Tropic of Capricorn

Tropic of Capricorn · Carnarvon · GREAT VICTORIA DESERT · South Australia · Lake Eyre · Brisbane

Geraldton · Cook · Darling R. · Bourke · PACIFIC OCEAN

Kalgoorlie · Port Augusta · Broken Hill · New South Wales · Sydney

Perth · Great Australian Bight · Port Lincoln · Adelaide · Murray R. · Canberra · Australian Capital Territory

Victoria · Melbourne

Tasmania · Tasman Sea · Hobart

N E S W

Scale: 0 – 250 – 500 miles / 0 – 250 – 500 kilometers

A

Rainfall Map of Australia

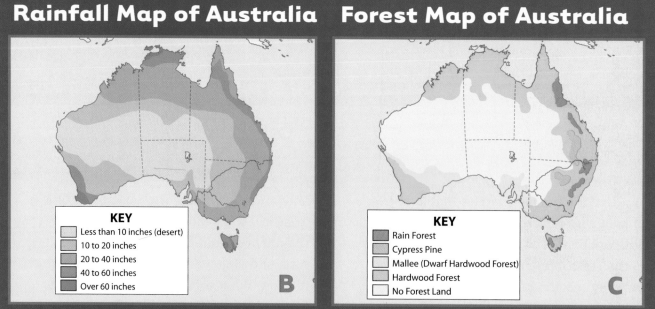

KEY
- ☐ Less than 10 inches (desert)
- ☐ 10 to 20 inches
- ☐ 20 to 40 inches
- ☐ 40 to 60 inches
- ☐ Over 60 inches

B

Forest Map of Australia

KEY
- ☐ Rain Forest
- ☐ Cypress Pine
- ☐ Mallee (Dwarf Hardwood Forest)
- ☐ Hardwood Forest
- ☐ No Forest Land

C

Australia is both a continent and a country. Although it is the smallest of the seven continents, it is the sixth-largest nation in terms of land area. As of 2006, only about 20.2 million people live in Australia. Most live in large cities located on the continent's eastern and southeastern coasts. Australia is divided into six states and two territories.

Think It Over

1. Map A shows the location of Australia's major cities. Which other map helps explain the location of these cities? How does this map help explain the location of these cities?

2. Australia is nicknamed "the land down under." Why do you think this might be? What information on these maps could help explain the nickname?

Use Your Skills

Fill in the answers to the following questions. Then indicate which map or maps on page 36 you used to find the answers — A, B, or C?

1. Which states have their capitals on the Pacific Ocean? _____
   _____ Map or maps used: _____

2. Which state would you live in if you wanted to be close to the Great Barrier Reef? _____
   _____ Map or maps used: _____

3. Which Australian state is an island? _____
   _____ Map or maps used: _____

4. Australia is located entirely _____ of the equator. Map or maps used: _____

5. The state of _____ does not have desert areas. Map or maps used: _____

6. The city of Cook receives_____ inches of rain a year. Map or maps used: _____

7. The rainforests of Australia receive at least _____ inches of rain a year. Map or maps used: _____

8. The main type of forest in Tasmania is _____ . Map or maps used: _____

Great Barrier Reef, Queensland, Australia

Ayers Rock, Uluru-Kata Tjuta National Park, Australia

World Population

World Populaton Density

KEY

Persons per sq. mi.	Persons per sq. km.
Over 250	Over 100
125–250	50–100
25–125	10–50
2–25	1–10
Under 2	Under 1

The world's population in late 2006 was about 6.5 billion. The map above shows the world's population density, or how crowded it is in different areas. Use the map and the table of the world's most populous nations to answer the questions. Use other maps in this book if necessary.

Ten Most Populous Nations in the World, 2006

China	1.3 billion
India	1.1 billion
United States	300 million
Indonesia	232 million
Brazil	188 million
Pakistan	167 million
Bangladesh	147 million
Russia	142 million
Nigeria	132 million
Japan	127 million

Use Your Skills

1. What part of China has the greatest population density? _____

2. What is the most populous country in South America? _____

3. Which part of the United States has a higher population density, the eastern or western part? _____

4. Which U.S. state has the largest amount of area with less than 2 people per square mile? _____

5. What land region in Africa has very few people? _____

6. Which continent has the most nations in the top ten list? _____

World Rainfall

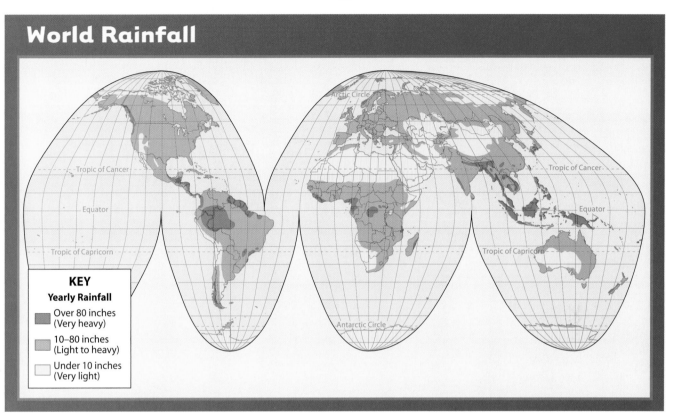

World Rainfall

KEY
Yearly Rainfall

- Over 80 inches (Very heavy)
- 10–80 inches (Light to heavy)
- Under 10 inches (Very light)

This rainfall map highlights areas of very heavy and very light rainfall around the world. Use this map, along with the population density map on page 38 and other maps in this book, to answer the following questions.

 Use Your Skills

1. Which region in the United States has a large area that receives less than 10 inches of rain a year? _____

2. How much rain do countries in northeastern South America receive each year? _____

3. How would you describe the rainfall in lands on or near the equator? _____
_____

4. Which country receives more rainfall, India or Egypt? _____

5. How would you describe the population density in the largest region of heavy rainfall in South America? _____

6. Circle each place below that has both very light rainfall and very low population density.
   a. southwest Africa   **d.** northern Spain
   b. southern Italy   **e.** eastern China
   c. central Australia

 Think It Over

The map above shows three rainfall categories. In which of these three regions are most of the world's most densely populated areas? How do you think rainfall affects where people live?

Endangered Rain Forests

World Rain Forests

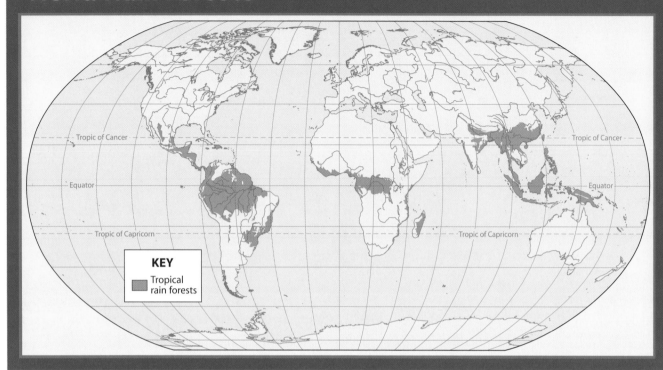

KEY

Tropical rain forests

The world's tropical rain forests are being destroyed at an alarming rate. Every second, about 1.4 acres are destroyed. Every day, an area larger than New York City is leveled. The rain forests have been cleared to provide land for cattle ranching, settlement, and developments such as hydroelectric dams and oil pipelines.

Rain forest destruction is a serious problem. Rain forests filter carbon dioxide, a gas that is formed in the atmosphere when fuel containing carbon is burned. Without the rain forests to filter the carbon dioxide, many scientists believe that global warming, a gradual increase in temperatures, will speed up. The results of global warming could be devastating. Deserts could spread, droughts could increase, icebergs and glaciers could melt. The levels of the oceans could rise, flooding coastal areas.

Facts About Rain Forests

- Rain forests cover about 6 percent of Earth's land. At one time, they covered at least twice that amount of land.

- Rain forests are home to about 30 million species of plants, animals, and insects.

- Rain forest destruction causes the extinction of 137 species each day.

- Plants found in rain forests are the sources of many important medicines. Most of the 3,000 plants identified by the National Cancer Institute as having potential anti-cancer properties are found only in rain forests.

- Most of Earth's rain forests will disappear by 2030 if their destruction continues at its current rate.

Amazon Rain Forest

Use Your Skills

1. Between what special lines of latitude are most of the world's rain forests located?

   _____

   _____

2. What nations have tropical rain forests in the Amazon region? _____

   _____

3. How many rain forest species become extinct during a one-year period? _____

4. In Africa, most rain forests are located just above or below the _____ .

5. Which African island nation has a large rain forest area? _____

6. Which regions of Asia have rain forests?

   _____

7. Which continents have no rain forests?

   _____

Think It Over

Which of the world's continents is not shown on this map? Do you think this continent has tropical rain forests? Explain your answer.

Your Turn Now

What can people do to help save our rain forests? Working with a small group, do Internet research to find out what some people are doing. Then form an action plan summarizing what you and your group can do to help preserve rain forests. Present your plan to the class.

Using a Time Zone Map

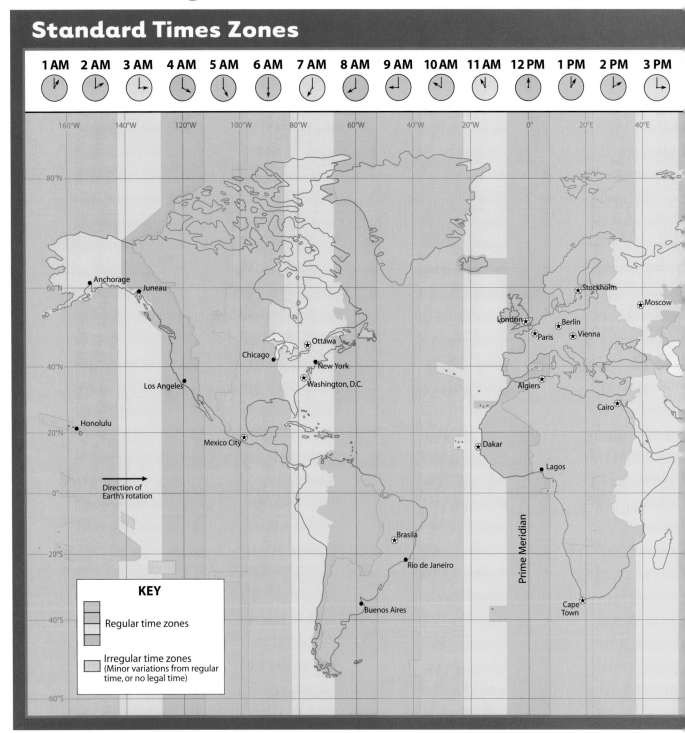

Standard Times Zones

1 AM	2 AM	3 AM	4 AM	5 AM	6 AM	7 AM	8 AM	9 AM	10 AM	11 AM	12 PM	1 PM	2 PM	3 PM

160°W   140°W   120°W   100°W   80°W   60°W   40°W   20°W   0°   20°E   40°E

80°N

60°N Anchorage Juneau

Stockholm
Moscow
London Berlin
Paris Vienna

40°N Chicago Ottawa
New York
Los Angeles Washington, D.C.
Algiers
Cairo

Honolulu
20°N
Mexico City
Dakar

Lagos

0° Direction of
Earth's rotation

Brasília
20°S
Rio de Janeiro

Prime Meridian

Cape
Town

KEY

Regular time zones

Irregular time zones
(Minor variations from regular
time, or no legal time)

40°S Buenos Aires

60°S

Earth rotates on its axis as it revolves around the sun, making sunrise and sunset occur at different times in different parts of the world. To avoid confusion, most of the world's countries have agreed upon a system of standard time zones. The different-colored bands on the map above show the 24 time zones into which Earth is divided. Each time zone represents one hour in the 24-hour day. As you can see on the map, the time in each zone is later as you move from west to east. New York,

6 PM	7 PM	8 PM	9 PM	10 PM	11 PM	12 AM

Map labels: 100°E, 120°E, 140°E, 160°E, 180°

80°, 60°, 40°, 20°, 0°, 20°, 40°, 60°

Beijing, Tokyo, Shanghai, bai (ay), Manila, International Date Line, Canberra, Sydney, Wellington, Monday / Sunday

for example, is one time zone east of Chicago. So the time in New York is one hour later than it is in Chicago. Los Angeles is two time zones west of Chicago. So the time in Los Angeles is two hours earlier than it is in Chicago.

✴ Use Your Skills

1. When it is noon in London, it is _____ a.m. in New York City.

2. When it is noon in Berlin, it is _____ in Ottawa.

3. When it is 2 p.m. in Cairo, it is _____ p.m. in the capital of France.

4. Mexico City is in the same time zone as the city of _____ in the United States.

5. What African city shown on the map is in the same time zone as Vienna? _____

_____

6. When it is 8 a.m. in the capital of the United States, it is _____ in the capital of Canada.

7. When it is noon in New York, what time is it in Los Angeles? _____

8. When it is 6 a.m. in Rio de Janeiro, what time is it in Moscow? _____

9. You have a friend in Manila, the Philippines. She wants you to call her on Wednesday at 9 a.m. Manila time. You live in Chicago. What day and time will it be in Chicago when you call your friend? _____

_____

10. Find the time zone you live in on this map. If it is 8 p.m. in Paris, what time will it be in your community? _____

Review

 **Map It!**

This is a blank map of the world. Using what you have learned from the maps in this book, fill in important information on this blank map. Be sure to:

- Draw and label the equator and prime meridian.

- Label the Atlantic Ocean, Pacific Ocean, Indian Ocean.

- Label at least 20 countries.

- Label at least 5 other places. They could be continents, countries, cities, or other geographic features.

- Label at least 10 cities.

- Label your own town or city.

- Give your map a title.

Review
Comparing Maps

South America, Political

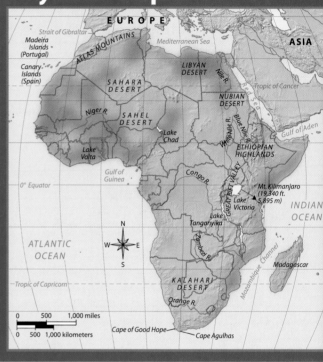

Physical Map of Africa

Comparing Maps

To answer questions 1—6 below, look at the maps above.

1. Which map shows what the land is like on a continent?

_____

2. What kind of map is it?

_____

3. Which map is a political map?

_____

4. What does a political map show?

_____

_____

5. Where in this book can you find a political map of the area shown on the physical map above?

_____

6. What other kinds of maps can you find in this book?

_____

_____

Finding Information

Look through your book to find a map that will help you locate each piece of information listed below. Write the name of the map, its page number, and the answer.

1. Where most explorers who reached the South Pole began their routes

_____

_____

_____

2. U.S. cities with a population of more than 1 million

_____

_____

_____

_____

3. The line of latitude that passes through Oslo, Norway

_____

_____

4. The meridian that passes through Aden, Yemen

_____

_____

5. The largest country that used to be part of the Soviet Union

_____

_____

6. Whether Europe or northern Africa gets more rainfall in a year

_____

_____

7. A city where it is the same time as in Paris, France

_____

_____

_____

Notes